# Building Habits

Pradip N Das

Published by Pradip Narayan Das, 2022.

# Also by Pradip N Das

**Success Plan for Youth**
Teenagers' Guide To Success

**Standalone**
Success Strategy for Students
Seven Essential Skills to Success
The Power of Attitude in Success
Building Mental Strength For Success
7 Best Sacrifices To Success
The Art of Managing Success
The Power of Reading
Steps to Design Your Life
Building Habits

# Table of Contents

# BUILDING HABITS

Step By Step Methods To Develop A Strong Foundation, Increase Productivity, Reduce Anxiety And Build Success Mindset To Grow Fast.

# PRADIP N DAS

## Download Another Book for Free

I want to thank you for buying my book and offer you another book (just as valuable as this one): *The Art of Managing Success*, completely free.

CLICK HERE[1]

---

# Your Attention Please

# Introduction

*"Success does not come from what you do occasionally, it comes from what you do consistently" - Marie Forleo*

Tina has a goal to learn to speak French; she spends at least 30 minutes learning French every day. She decides that early morning is the best time to learn French, so she resolves to go to bed early to wake up at 6:00 AM. She uploads some French learning podcasts onto her laptop. She listens every night while making dinner. After some time, she realizes that she's forgetting some of the words she's learning through podcasts. She knows that she remembers more when she makes notes, so she starts writing new words and their meanings down in a notebook.

When Tina tells her friend about her goal, she agrees to talk French with her every day. Tina feels more energized about reaching her goal now that her friend is supporting her, and she has a new opportunity to practice what she's learning. In return, Tina helps her to improve her English.

Here Tina is trying to achieve her goal by building good habits.

Committing to habits allows you to free up your brain capacity to make better decisions, do your best work when you are in a prime mental state, and stay on track even when things are difficult. This way, development happens.

Habits can make or ruin our fortunes. They actually form the foundation of our character and destiny. It is easy to acquire bad and evil habits but challenging to cultivate and acquire good ones. Habits, once acquired, are challenging to get rid of. Habits become part and parcel of one's nature and behavior. We are the makers or destroyers of our destiny. Because we cultivate, practice, and acquire good or bad habits and their fruits accordingly. One may have a bad habit of flattering others or making false promises. Similarly, one may have a bad habit of stealing things. One habit leads to another, and then there is a sort of chain of habits from which an escape is impossible, particularly in advanced age.

Anything done often and repeatedly becomes a habit; the force of habit is compelling. The more we repeat and practice anything, the easier, permanent, and automatic it becomes. If we do not practice and repeat a habit, we feel uneasy and uncomfortable. Take, for example, the habit of taking tea. There are people who consume umpteen numbers of cups of tea daily. They may do without food, newspapers, or rest but cannot dispense with hot cups of tea taken almost every hour of the day. They will feel sick, lethargic, bored, and useless without enjoying their cups of tea. The same is the case with smokers or drunkards. Habits are too forceful to be avoided. The constant and repeated use and practice give birth to a habit. There cannot be any habit without constant and repeated use and frequency.

There are many forces and factors that play an essential role in forming habits. Early education, impressions, influences, company, associations, etc., are some of the significant factors in forming habits.

For example, a boy who sees his father smoking is very likely to cultivate this evil habit. The boy may imagine that there must be some joy, excitement, and thrill in the habit; that is why his father indulged in it. One day he may try it stealthily as smoking material is easily available in the home. Gradually he may become a habitual smoker and spread it among his friends and associates.

# Habits-The Foundation of Success

There is a story that when the great library of Alexandria was burned, one book was saved. But it was not a valuable book, and so a poor man, who could read a little, bought it for a few coppers. It was not very interesting, yet there was a most exciting thing in it. It was a thin strip of vellum on which the secret of the "touchstone" was written.

The touchstone was a small pebble that could turn any common metal into pure gold. The writing explained that it was on the shores of the Black Sea, lying among thousands and thousands of other pebbles which looked exactly the same. But the secret was this: the real stone would feel warm, while ordinary pebbles are cold. So the man sold his few belongings, bought some simple supplies, camped on the seashore, and began testing the pebbles.

This was his plan: he knew that if he picked up ordinary pebbles and threw them down again because they were cold, he might pick up the same pebbles hundreds of times. So when he felt a cold one, he threw it into the sea. He spent a whole day doing this, and none of them was the touchstone. Then he spent a week, a month, a year, three years... but he did not find the touchstone. Yet he went on and on this way: pick up a pebble, it's cold, throw it into the sea... and so on and so on. Just visualize the man doing it for years and years and years — pick up a pebble, it is cold, throw it into the sea... from morning to evening, for years and years.

But one morning, he picked up a pebble, and it was WARM — and he threw it into the sea. You should understand that he had formed the habit of throwing them into the sea, and habit made him do it when he finally found the touchstone, poor fellow. [1]

Habits make us who we are. Everything that you achieve in life is due to your habits. Therefore, change your habits if you do not get the desired results. In other words, habits will either make you or break you. Habits shape our lives far more than we probably realize. Habits are powerful. It is said that more than forty percent of the actions a person performs each day are not actual decisions but habits. The habits grow stronger and stronger over time and become more and more automatic. So make sure you have developed the right habits which make life easier.

Habits may be something you do every now and then. A good example is brushing of teeth in the morning; you will not feel good if you do not brush your teeth after getting up in the morning. This is the automated activity or a habit we all possess.

A habit is more like an addiction to certain things, which can be either good or bad and is often very hard to let go of but not impossible. A habit can change a man's behavior, lifestyle, perception, approach, etc., Any kind of habit builds up a character/image for a person irrespective of their physical appearance.

A habit is a tendency to do something, whether harmful or beneficial. A good habit will help you reach your goals, develop personally and professionally, and feel fulfilled, whereas a bad habit may completely ruin your life.

Habits have a compounding impact. They seem to make little difference initially or on a particular day, but the impact they deliver over a period of time is enormous. It multiplies over a while.

It doesn't matter how successful or unsuccessful you are right now. What matters is whether your habits are putting you on the path toward success. Samuel Beckett said, "Life is a habit. Or rather, life is a succession of habits."

Our habit also determines how happy and fulfilled we will become in the future. I've seen many talented and potential successful persons who ended their life's journey with regret and unhappiness because of persisting in bad habits.

Habits are a double-edged sword. They can work for you or against you. Habits are overlearned modes of behavior. When someone starts giving the same response to the same stimuli over time, they form a habit. I think when people start doing something just to derive pain from it, it becomes an addiction. There is a strong negative charge attached to pain; habit is more neutral in nature.

Good and bad habits are your lifestyle. Good habits are an ornament, and the bad is a curse. Rising early, speaking the truth, honesty, reading books, and goodwill are among the good habits that make us shine in our performance, form a good reputation for us, and help us become successful in every field of life. Bad habits like smoking, drinking, lying, stealing, and gambling give us a timely pleasure but ruin us in the long run. They earn us a bad name and put us in trouble. The habits or the repetitive things you do in life will change some even if you don't plan it that way, and it is your responsibility to try and make good habits dominate more of your lifestyle when changes are made. Good habits usually refer to your moral conduct and your way of living. It is the way you treat others and behave with them. Being polite and considerate toward others is considered a good habit. If you meet others with a smile and treat everyone with respect, you have good social habits.

Wikipedia defines them as "a routine of behavior that is repeated regularly and tends to occur subconsciously." The Merriam-Webster Dictionary defines habits as "an acquired mode of behavior that has become nearly or completely involuntary." Stanford Professor, social scientist, and Tiny Habits author BJ Fogg describes habits this way: "When it comes to behavior, decision and habit are opposites. Decisions require deliberation; habits do not." In "The Power of Habit," author Charles Duhigg adds automaticity. "Simply put, a habit is a behavior that starts as a choice and then becomes a nearly unconscious pattern." According to Atomic Habits author James Clear, "habits are the small decisions you make and actions you perform every day."

What once starts as a conscious decision becomes unconscious. This is the defining characteristic of all habits, whether atomic, tiny, minor or any other size.

The main benefit of habits is that they require little conscious thought. You can use those extra cycles to make other decisions. Effective habits make you more efficient. Some general habits are vital such as eating, drinking, walking, communicating, and sleeping. What you eat, drink, and communicate is subject to some change to improve those habits and exclude any bad ones you may have. Most habits are somewhat impulsive and not easily changeable, and an awareness of what habits you have is the first step towards improving them if that is what you want to do.

To change habits, you can decrease or increase the time spent on them, change the composition of the habits, and exclude or change habits or introduce new ones.

Bad habits are difficult to change since you are probably getting some satisfaction out of them, so first, decreasing the time spent on them is frequently a wise choice. Totally and quickly, excluding a bad habit may be necessary for a crisis situation. Still, the intelligent thing to do is gradually reduce the time spent on a bad habit.

What do you replace the bad habit with? A good habit may mean increasing the time spent on a good habit or introducing a new good habit to replace some or all of the old bad habit.

Prioritizing your life goals will help you decide what you want to do more of and what you would like to decrease in your life gradually.

While addictive bad habits like gambling, pornography, promiscuity, excessive impulsive shopping, drugs, and alcohol need profound change, your most important priority is healthy eating and drinking, including more and more organic food and drink into your daily habits. Get plenty of sleep and a little exercise, and you are well on your way to a healthy body which is the foundation of a healthy mind too.

To improve the health of your mind and keep it from stagnating with old habitual thoughts, learn new valuable skills and new valuable knowledge, which means spending time researching and reading something useful as frequently as possible.

Bad friends and unhealthy relationships are also bad habits that can decrease your health and happiness, so consider decreasing the time spent with them. If you have bad relationships with offspring and spouse and you are mostly to blame for this situation, then seriously try to change your behavior or call it quits and get a divorce and exit the family with your unchanging bad personality.

Good habits are just as addictive as bad habits so try to stay addicted to the good ones for more excellent health and happiness in your life.

**Difference between Habits and Routines**

Habit and a routine both are regular, repeated actions. But while habits run on autopilot through the subconscious mind whereas routines are intentional. Routines need deliberate practice and effort. But a habit happens with little or no conscious thought.

For instance, daily exercise requires intention and effort. It won't run automatically. The same is true for gratitude. You're not going to start gratitude on autopilot.

Unlike habits, routines are uncomfortable and require a concerted effort. Waking up early to run every morning or meditating for 10 minutes every night, for instance, are rituals that initially are hard to keep up. On the other hand, habits are so ingrained in our daily lives that it feels strange not to do them. Imagine not brushing your teeth immediately after getting up or not drinking a cup of tea with breakfast. If these are habits you have already formed, avoiding them might even feel bad.

For a routine to become a habit, the behavior will need to happen with little or no thought. For instance, let's say you add drinking green juice to your morning routine. You can consider it a habit if you wake up and make green juice every day without thinking about it. But if it requires effort to make green juice, it is routine.

15

# Habits and Self-Discipline

Many times you decide something, and you are unable to follow through. Many times you justify yourself about your inactions and indecisions. For example, you decide to do meditation every morning and sincerely start for a few days. After a few days or a week, the problem starts. You start thinking of the excuse, like, "I should probably sleep 5 minutes more. It's okay even if I am late for 5 minutes". "I slept a little late last night, and if I don't get enough sleep, I won't be able to be productive at work today." "I am not feeling well today." "Mood is not there." "I will compensate for today and do in the evening." etc., etc.

You think, become a defaulter, and then you justify. You hide against your excuses with rationality and logic. It makes you feel good about yourself that you have justified your excuses. All these internal dialogues lead to inaction.

Many people understand and acknowledge the importance of self-discipline but are not able to implement it. Self-discipline is the key to developing habits. Any habit to develop, whether small or big, requires a high level of self-discipline. Many try for this and leave after a few days. Others feel that it is too harsh, not their cup of tea, and therefore, they do not make any effort to get it.

Self-discipline is vital. It would not be wrong to say that without self-discipline development of good habits are not possible. People who live disciplined life make sure that they sleep on time and sleep enough every day. They get up early and take better charge of their day. They understand the importance of exercise and are engaged regularly. They have complete self-control and do not give in to temptation. On the other hand, those who lack self-discipline are inconsistent and looser. They are not self-controlled and easily tempted.

Self-discipline helps to develop good habits such as healthy eating habits. A self-disciplined person understands the importance of good habits, so he always goes for building good habits. For example, a person who eats healthy food can take better charge of his day and feel in control. He remains energetic throughout the day and gives a better chance to fulfill his goals. On the other hand, those who eat oily and sugar foods feel lethargic and out of control. They feel very little energy and are very tired of fulfilling their goals.

# The Power of Habits

A wealthy businessman had a son who had many bad habits. The wealthy man requested a wise man to help his son get rid of his bad habits. The wise man asked the son to take a walk with him through the garden. After walking a few steps, the wise man stopped and asked the young man to pluck a small flower out of the ground.

The young man grabbed the plant with his fingers and quickly plucked it out. The wise man nodded, and they resumed walking.

A few seconds later, the wise man stopped again and pointed towards another plant, a bit larger than the previous one. The young man grabbed it with his hand and plucked it out of the ground with a bit of effort. "Now pluck out that one," the wise man said, pointing towards a bush. The young man gripped the bush with both of his hands, and using all of his strength, he managed to pluck it out of the ground.

"Now you see that small tree, there? Try and pluck that one." The young man grabbed the trunk with both hands and pulled as hard as he could, but he couldn't even move it.

"It's impossible. I can't do it."

"You see, my boy, it's the same with our habits. If we let them grow and take root, it becomes harder and harder for us to stop them."

I set my new year resolutions and never fulfilled them like millions of people for years. But very recently, I have understood the power of habits. This is the hard truth that we are a result of our habits. Successful people have developed the proper habits that lead to excellence. Our discipline should focus on building the new habit, not controlling or taking over the bad habits. Like the Space Shuttle, willpower and discipline work like rocket boosters that run long enough for a habit to kick in and take over. Discipline is an effective habit, and effective habits lead to practical results. Conversely, ineffective habits produce ineffective results.

The importance of habit is just as great in forming moral character as in training soldiers and horses to show obedience to the word of command. All moralists recognize the fact that it is possible for men to become better or worse by the cultivation of good or bad habits; in fact, it is just this that makes moral progress and deterioration possible. A man who yields to temptation may at first do so with reluctance. Still, after yielding once or twice, resistance becomes more difficult until, at last, by continuing submission, he is wholly enslaved and has no control over his evil passions. On the contrary, if he had conquered the first temptation, his will would have thereby become stranger. After frequent victories, he would have been so habituated to self-control that the temptation, which had first tried him, would have lost attractive power. Then he might have led his moral will, strengthened by the habit of victory, to still greater moral efforts.

**Good Habits are for a better life**

Habits are the foundation for personal development, and personal development is the key to success. Developing better habits helps us to follow discipline in our lives. But where do habits come from, and how are they developed? And why is it that when we try to change our habits, we only follow through for so long before we give up and revert to our old ways?

If you can follow better habits in your everyday life, the bad ones tend to slip away. This takes discipline and won't be easy, but self-discipline becomes more effortless as you stick with it like any self-betterment.

There's no confusion over how to discipline yourself when you work on embodying the best possible habits for your own life. Habits take time, whether you're making them or breaking them. Start small, work consistently, and make sure always to build, and the way forward will always be completely clear to you.

# Habits Determine Your Future

Everyone on this planet wants to be successful. But, the question arises of how to achieve success? If you believe in yourself and if you think you can, everything is possible. But, you need to understand that your success depends on your habits. If you have good habits, success will be there waiting for you. Most successful people make some self-induced rules as we all know that success doesn't come by accident or coincidence. So, most successful people choose to develop good habits and get rid of their bad habits.

Success may be defined as achieving the desired outcome or accomplishing particular aims or goals in different spheres of life. Naturally, it is common for people to wish to be successful in their lives. Success is a condition that is often achieved through the mediation of such tools as individual habits and attitudes. Good habits are essential to being successful in life. A person with good habits makes steady progress in studies, career, personal life, and all. On the other hand, a person with bad habits, however talented he/she is, will one day lose success in life.

Duhigg advocates the significance of the processes that occur in the human brain whilst attempting to achieve success. Duhigg concentrates on the issue of habits and the exchange of negative habits for more positive ones.

**Impact on Personal life**

Habits make or break life. If some one desires to work for personal development, the first thing he/she should do is replace his/her bad habits with good habits and bring discipline in life. Once a person starts developing good habits, he is improving himself.

Habits are essential to living a good life. They can make or break your chances of achieving and maintaining your lifestyle goals such as mediation, good eating plan, physical exercise, work planning, etc. Bad habits like increased consumption of sugary soft drinks and fast food and low activity levels are linked to the development of chronic diseases such as obesity and diabetes. On the flip side, maintaining healthy habits, such as eating plenty of fruit, vegetables, and fresh foods and exercising regularly, can benefit health. Healthy habits can help us achieve ideal weights, keep blood sugars in range and help lower the risk of diseases like diabetes and cancer.

Research says the best way to bring change into your life is by creating new routines and sticking to them until they become habits. The way to make sure we cultivate the new behavior is to reward ourselves. With motivation, we repeat the action repeatedly until it becomes ingrained.

I've found that the best way to achieve your goals is by committing to a new healthy habit. By definition, a habit is a regular tendency that's difficult to give up. When you create healthy habits that are difficult to give up, you will inevitably get closer to achieving your bigger goals.

Harnessing the power of habits is a great way to pursue success. Committing to habits allows you to free up your brain capacity to make better decisions, do your best work when you are in a prime mental state, and stay on track even when things are difficult.

Habits play a role of paramount importance in simplifying our lives. We as humans make a lot of small to big decisions in our daily life, and all our choices and decisions require some amount of mental energy. We get susceptible to fatigue since this energy is finite during the day. That is where habits come in and play an important role because you do not have to choose or train your mind all over again to perform actions— you just do it.

Habits are encoded in the structures of our brain that helps us save a lot of effort because we do not have to relearn everything we do. They help to create routine, order, and efficiency. This automation of your actions leaves ample energy at your disposal that can be used to focus on other tasks.

**Impact on Professional life**

Developing positive habits for the workplace can help you achieve career goals, maximize your productivity, and remain focused on the task. It's essential to develop and maintain good work habits. If consistently maintained, good work habits drive success, resulting in an employee contributing more, increasing their job satisfaction while creating healthy relationships between colleagues, up and down the line team.

A solid foundation of good work habits is required to maximize work efficiency, productivity, reliability, and teamwork. Basic work habits can include cooperation, effective communication, following policy, organization, punctuality, regular attendance, and time management. Employees who utilize good work habits can extend their regular job duties and tasks by assisting their peers in an auxiliary role to optimize company efficiency and productivity to meet the bottom line.

How you operate in your workplace can impact your productivity and career success. It can also affect your relationships with others on your team, including co-workers and managers. It's important to establish working habits that will help contribute to a cohesive work environment that benefits all employees. Whether you're working at a large multinational company, an emerging start-up, or a small business, exhibiting great work habits is key to impressing your business manager and boosting your career. Regardless of how long you have been in your field, the principles are to act professionally, show interest, and work hard.

**Impact in Society**

Habits help in predicting someone's future. The impact of a good habit is a success, while that of a bad habit is a failure. Success is not magical and hence follows principles and processes. Good habits influence and attract people to you, whereas bad habit repels the good ones. The kind of persons we attract also determines the level of success or failure attached to it.

If society benefits from your habits, then nothing is better than that. For example, suppose you practice yoga or meditation daily, and people of your society, your groups, or your friends and families get inspired by your habits and develop similar habits. In that case, you are contributing to society directly. Similarly, if you have achieved something good in sports or any area because of your good habits, people definitely get encouraged to develop similar habits. It has an immense impact on the overall development of society and the country as a whole.

# How Dangerous The Bad Habits Are

Every person has some kind of bad habit. The impact can be varied based on the types of bad habits, from small, non-dangerous habits like biting nails or high pitched laughing to dangerous ones such as smoking, drinking, and reckless behavior. Habits can go unnoticed by people because they vary in seriousness. Breaking habits vary greatly. It can be as simple as not doing something in the morning to stop drugs and alcohol. People often pick up bad habits in their younger years. Some habits people cannot control, such as getting angry quickly or an outburst. But most of the habits people are able to overcome and control.

Some people smoke, some binge eats, and some might even engage in self-destructive behavior. These habits are often deeply ingrained into one's personality, to the point of becoming the traits by which many define themselves. If you want to change the course of your life, you have to learn how to change these bad habits. Although it is an often long and challenging process, the results will allow you to succeed where you may have otherwise failed. The steps below can help you learn how to identify, confront and eventually eliminate the habits that might control your life.

Bad habits are just a part of our day-to-day life. Your bad habits are often part of who you are. You might make excuses for them, embrace them or even get a bit prickly when others bring them up. In reality, though, these are not just habits—they are a failure. They might be holding you back from achieving success in business, your social life, or even love. Embracing your bad habits means simply learning how to live with what is going wrong, but eliminating them means that you are willing to make a positive change in your own life. There is nothing that says that this is easy, of course, but you should be willing to try it.

Bad habits are hard to get rid of once they have settled in our system. It is best to get rid of them early on, or they should be nipped in the bud. You can understand this by the following example. Imagine a person who starts to smoke. He isn't probably not going to catch lung cancer after smoking his first cigarette. However, if he keeps this consistent habit for many years, there is a much bigger risk of getting cancer. The problem lies here: these habits initially look harmless, but they'll grow into big proportions over time. When you overlook the power of small actions or decisions, that's when the negative side-effects start to kick in – sooner or later.

I realized this with my bad eating habits, and once I understood what I was doing, I had to change my lifestyle for good. Some of those bad habits are not simply bad; they are worse. Knowingly or unknowingly, they take away our healthy lifestyle from us. But we cannot understand that unless we reach the end spot. Ultimately, then there would be nothing left for us to do.

A person having one dangerous bad habit can negate hundreds of his good habits and completely demolish their life. Low-intensity bad habits can be manageable, and even if it stays, the impact will not be so dangerous or destructive.

# Common Habits of Successful People

*"Success does not come from what you do occasionally, it comes from what you do consistently" - Marie Forleo*

When it comes to habits, I am one of the biggest believers that habits make us who we are. Everything that you achieve in life is due to your habits. Therefore, if you do not like the results you are getting, change your habits. In other words, habits will either make you or break you, so be sure to play smart. To be able to do so, you need to work hard to develop many good habits in life. This does not necessarily mean you should turn your life around, but you can start small and move from there.

Habits shape our lives far more than we probably realize. Habits are powerful. Our brains cling to them at the exclusion of all else—including common sense. It is said that more than forty percent of the actions a person performs each day are not actual decisions but habits. The habits grow stronger and stronger over time and become more and more automatic. So make sure you have developed the right habits.

Successful people bear several common good habits. If you can develop these habits today, that will completely change your life for the better:-

1.  Get up early

You must have heard the popular saying, "Early to bed, early to rise makes a person healthy, wealthy, and wise." When you wake up early in the morning, you feel refreshed, happier and active. Since there is less disturbance and noise in the morning and our mind is fresh, we can concentrate more on our studies and work.

By waking up early, you can do yoga, meditation, exercise, or go for a walk on a routine basis. By doing so, we will feel fitter and healthier. Along with health advantages, waking up early also has some mental benefits. It reduces our stress and anger, changes our attitude to optimism, and helps us achieve success in our lives.

There are various benefits and advantages of early rising. Early rising is the first step to success. The advantage of early rising is the good start it gives us in our day's work. The early riser completes a large amount of work before other people get out of their bed. Rising early refreshes our mind and body. Morning is the best time of the day. The work done at that time is done well as there are a few sounds or distractions. One of the significant advantages of early rising is having breakfast on time. Breakfast is the most important meal of the day, and it plays a significant role in our lives. People, who start their work early, do better than those who start late. An early riser is not tempted to hurry as he has plenty of time to do the work. All of his work gets finished in good time. He is left with enough free time which he could do some other work or some leisure activities. So, promise yourself to get up early and develop the habit of early rising. Early rising is a boon, so bless yourself with it!

Waking up can be one of the most difficult challenges for some people. But for some of the most successful people in art, business, and sports, early rising is key to their success.

You may be surprised to know that Apple CEO Tim Cook, Oprah Winfrey, Michelle Obama, and Indra Nooyi have been known to rise at the crack of dawn. Early morning gives you more time before rushing into a busy day with work, people, and stress, and it is the most precious time of the day. There is a certain magic about the mornings. The world hasn't woken up yet, there is no stress on the outside and everything, and it is the only time that you are not bothered by anyone or anything else. Use that time, refresh in that time and do something that makes you feel like you accomplished something already. There is no more powerful motivator than having finished something important before the rest of the world even wakes up!

1.  Physical Exercise

Medical professionals usually recommend adequate exercise, sleep, and feeding as the key requirements of being healthy. But unfortunately, exercise happens to be one of such aspects of human activities that people pay little or zero attention to.

One thing that most successful people have in common is an uncompromising attitude about fitness and exercise. This is because fitness can instill in you the fundamental building blocks necessary for achieving success. It is safe to say that if you cannot commit yourself to regular exercise, you will likely never reach your full potential. From Fortune 500 CEOs to entrepreneurs and celebrities, countless successful people have discovered the undeniable connection between fitness and success. This is partly because regular exercise enhances your physical and mental state, which lifts all other areas of your life as well. In addition, fitness builds a fundamental knowledge base of the mindset you must cultivate to achieve anything that seems out of reach.

Your body is made to move, not to stand still, so find every possible way to move your body as much as you can during the day. The benefits of physical exercise are enormous. Bodily exercise profited greatly. It fosters sound health. Exercising every day boosts energy, reduces the risk of chronic diseases, uplifts your mood, increases productivity, and the most important is that it keeps you fit. It keeps your body fit for your day-to-day activities. It keeps your body serviced. When an engine is overused without regular servicing, it breaks down. Physical exercise is one such means of servicing the body. Making it your daily habit will keep you fit and healthy to live a better life.

1.  Set daily goals

Successful people "think" success all the time. That is why their goals are firmly lodged in their subconscious.

While most believe that having a long-term goal is crucial to success, successful people understand that you will get demotivated easily; success will become hard without small, daily goals.

The subconscious is brilliant at prioritizing. It listens to you and gauges what you think is the most important task from your thoughts. This means that what you think about most of the time is what the subconscious will think is the most important thing for you and try to find creative solutions.

If you think about problems, the subconscious will try to find you more problems. If you think about solutions, goals, and dreams, you will try to make them come true. But the subconscious goes even further when trying to understand what you think is important; it "listens" to your feelings.

Luckily, it has been proven that a positive thought is over 100 times as positive as a negative thought. This makes it a lot easier to drive positive emotions into your subconscious. It is enough to be positive and keep your thoughts on what you want — and you don't have to go monitoring your thoughts all the time.

1.  Reading

Many well-known personalities like Einstein, King of the share market Warren Buffet, and Amazon king Jeff Bezos claim to spend part of their busy day reading meaningful books, at least 500 pages. Elon Musk claims to have gained all his physics and rocket science knowledge solely from the vast books he read. Shashi Tharoor was once asked the secret of his first-to-be-heard words, to which he gave a hilarious reply.

Reading is supposed to arouse the imagination of readers. Books act as medicine for the broken mind, overcome traumas, and more. But one must be careful of the books they read. Everything on the planet has its pros and cons, and so does reading. Reading unwanted information can poison one's mind, so it's imperative to stay away from such books and dispose of the information gained.

Reading helps to broaden our horizons of subjects and also our vocabulary. A person with limited vocabulary tends to retreat into a shell at social gatherings. But a voracious reader can share an active part in such conversations besides adding to the information. Reading is beneficial for upcoming writers or bloggers as it is of utmost importance to them to use the precise words associated with their subjects. Reading also helps to express your ideas and thoughts precisely and clearly. To be a prolific writer, one should be a voracious reader. Reading will help ideas to flow into the right choice of words seamlessly. Not using precise words can easily bore the readers leading to the end of a career before taking off.

Reading is also a stress buster, which is similar to meditation. Life can present several stress factors in your daily life, like presenting, promoting, or preparing for an interview. Spending some quiet time in the morning reading your favorite book can relieve you and find yourself at peace in the most stressful of situations. Books can be your life companion.

Reading helps you leverage other people's experiences. Experience is the best teacher, but it must not be your experience. Make other person's experience your teacher by going through their books and materials.

Reading keeps you ahead of others. When you know what people don't know, it automatically places you on a higher pedestal. Reading sharpens your understanding. It sharpens your perception of things. It changes your view about people and things.

1. Keep a daily journal

In his book "7 Habits of Highly Successful People", Stephen Covey says about journaling, *Writing is another powerful way to sharpen the mental saw. Keeping a journal of our thoughts, experiences, insights, and learnings promotes mental clarity, exactness, and context.*"

A journal is an excellent tool for setting new goals, planning, and looking back at your accomplishments. You can chart your successes and failures daily. This makes it easy to look and see what's working and what's not working as you set new goals.

Keeping a journal and writing down your thoughts and ideas is one of the most powerful tools any successful executive has. Keeping a journal gets those great ideas, the long list of to-dos, your wishes, and your desires out of the back of your head. But many executives don't journal because it feels like a waste of time. They already feel they don't have enough time, but they don't realize that journaling saves time.

Every year millions of people set out to establish their New Year's Resolutions. The problem, most people fail within the first two weeks of the year. Why? Because they don't focus on creating a goal worth setting. Goals need to be identified, and if we can put a face to those goals, they can be visualized. The purpose of smarter goals is to make sure that we create specific goals. We will fail every time if we're not specific and don't take the time to figure out how to be specific.

But when you take the time each day to connect with your yearly goals by writing your next steps in a journal, you'll discover you can accomplish more than you initially thought.

Stephen Covey said, "Things which matter most must never be at the mercy of things which matter least." If your goals matter to you, write them down and revisit them daily.

1.  Focus thinking

Successful people focus on one thing at a time. They pick one thing and devote their time and energy to becoming great in that one area. Many of us take on too many goals at once, and we end up distracted and ultimately frustrated with ourselves. Therefore, pick one big goal over and above your regular commitments and devote all of your time, efforts, energy, and attention to doing your best for that goal.

Focus can bring energy and power to almost anything, whether physical or mental. If you're learning how to pitch a baseball and you want to develop a good curveball, then focused thinking while practicing will improve your technique. If you need to refine the manufacturing process of your product, focused thinking will help you develop the best method. If you want to solve a complex mathematics problem, focused thinking helps you break through to the solution. The greater the difficulty of a problem or issue, the more focused thinking time is necessary to solve it.

To take ideas to the next level, you must shift from being expansive in your thinking to being selective. I have discovered that a good idea can become a great idea when it is given focus time. Focusing on a single idea for a long time can indeed be very frustrating. I've often spent days focusing on thought and trying to develop it, only to find that I could not improve the idea. But sometimes, my perseverance in focused thinking pays off. That brings me great joy. And when focused thinking is at its best, not only does the idea grow, but so do I!

No one achieves greatness by becoming a generalist. You don't hone a skill by diluting your attention to its development. The only way to get to the next level is to focus. No matter whether your goal is to increase your level of play, sharpen your business plan, improve your bottom line, develop your subordinates, or solve personal problems, you need to focus. Author Harry A. Overstreet observed, "The immature mind hops from one thing to another; the mature mind seeks to follow through."

1.  Prioritize work

To get the most out of their to-do lists, all successful people prioritize tasks on their to-do lists. How does it help? Prioritization helps you understand which tasks are urgent, which tasks are complicated and require deep focus, and which tasks will take less/much time.

Also, successful people plan small, easy tasks first. Why? Finishing these tasks takes less time and energy, and crossing them off the lists gives them a sense of accomplishment that motivates them to complete the following tasks quickly.

So, if you want your to-do list to work for you, start prioritizing tasks. Believe me, my friends, your life will be a lot easier.

Stephen Covey uses the analogy of rocks, pebbles, and sand in a jar to make priorities understandable. First, if we fill a jar with sand (the least important task), there is no space for the rocks (the most important task). But if we begin by putting the big rocks first, we can adjust pebbles in between rocks, then pour in the sand on top, and we even can pour in some water before the jar is full.

Most of the time, we are not aware of the fact that we can avoid some tasks and could do other important tasks first. We are just not deciding on our priorities. If we do not compromise on worth-doing tasks, it will be easy for us to optimize our time correctly. We will get the best from our time.

You may have a large amount of work to do, but if you can't determine what is urgent and important, you will be in trouble. In order to manage your time correctly, the next step after preparing a to-do list is to prioritize your tasks where you choose what should be done first or immediately. Prioritizing helps you visually to see the highest to the lowest priority tasks.

1.  Visualize goal

Daily visualization of goals assists in accelerating the process of achieving the goals and makes the journey of the person most memorable. Visualization has a direct impact on strengthening the belief system of a person.

Visualization is a strong tool that reinforces your belief in yourself because this influences your behavior. If you see yourself as one of the best chess players in the world, or you see yourself as the future Olympic gold medalist in any sport, you will start behaving like that. So, you need to see yourself as someone worthy and unique. Visualization can help you create that image.

You can make a few affirmations such as you are the future gold medalist or future champion; you are working on that, making efforts to improve yourself to that level. If you visualize the process every day and affirm yourself, you will surely improve your self-belief.

1.  Fast Action Taker

Be it Leon Musk, Mukesh Ambani, or Alibaba; one thing is common—they never delay in taking action. Whatever good things they learn or come to their mind, they immediately implement them. If you do not take action, the idea will die, or learning will be replaced with another new learning; ultimately, the opportunity will be lost. Dreaming is essential to get the drive to do things, but ultimately you need to execute that. Execution is the key to converting the idea to the desired outcome. Action-oriented people never fail. The habit of taking action is the key to success.

Successful people are good at making decisions. They do not delay in making a decision and taking action. This does not mean they are making irresponsible decisions, but it is sometimes essential to take a risk, follow our intuition, and simply take action. It may not be perfect, but we keep on improvising and learning from our mistakes and correct them accordingly. Mistakes and failures are part of the game. Most successful people fail more than they win, but they never shy away from taking decisions and actions.

1.  Time Management

Time is flowing. You cannot hold it, catch it or buy it. Every person starts a new fresh day with 1440 minutes and no balance left at the end of the day. The only difference for successful people is that they consistently maximize each day's utilization productively. All truly successful people are great at managing the time they have available in their hands. They make every moment count, and they do not accept distractions or interruptions. They are exceptional planners and always try to stay organized.

Therefore, becoming successful in anything in your life is significantly connected to how organized you are and how well you manage your time.

1.  Learn a new thing

A lot of people stop learning and improving once they get into their first real job. They assume that they will stay on top of the game by just doing the bare minimum and then wonder why their life isn't changing for the better. Put in the time and effort. Invest in yourself.

Learning comes in different forms. It can be acquiring a new skill, gaining knowledge in your subject, learning a new language, strengthening your body and mind, etc.

Whenever you do something new, you find another dimension to your personality. You go deep within yourself and uncover aspects of your personality that will surprise you. You will start dwelling less and start doing more. Judgments will no longer scare you, and you will challenge your limits.

# How to Nurture Good Habits?

A lady came to a sage with the same question.

She said, "Guruji, how can I get rid of my bad habits?"

The sage asked her to bring him a cup of water from the river nearby. Though a little perplexed, she got the water from the river. The water was dirty.

Then, he asked her to take the clean water from the pot and keep pouring it onto the dirty water till the water became clean. The lady was very perplexed, but she still decided to indulge the sage.

She did as he said. Soon enough, after a few rounds of pouring clean water into the cup full of dirty water, the water in the cup became sparkling clean. She brought the cup to the sage.

The sage said, "Like the water in the cup which became clean after a few times of you pouring clean water from the pot, our bad habits need to be replaced by good ones."

Man can be said to be a bundle of habits. They may be good or bad. There cannot be a person only good or only evil. Speaking truth, frankness, honesty, service to others, cleanliness, reading good books, etc., are some of the good habits. Bad habits should be nipped in the bud, and good ones should be tried and practiced repeatedly, for they would die and perish for want of these.

When we are talking about habit forming, we actually talk about forming good habits. Habits forming is essential in life, but it is not so easy as it requires a lot of consistency over a long time and obviously patience. Habit-forming is the process in which behaviors become automatic. It can be an intentional process, or it can happen unplanned. For instance, you were most taught to wash your hands during childhood. And after a while, washing your hands became automatic. It wasn't intentional, but it happened after lots of repetition. One thing to keep in mind about the habit-forming process is that habit-forming is a long-term process and only happens when you become consistent in practicing the activity.

Habits and field paths are formed in the same way: by repetition. Villagers, as a rule, do not deliberately make a footpath to the next village. They just go the shortest or easiest way over the fields. Day after day, people go and come the same way. Their feet tread down the grass and beat the earth hard. Their repeated walking in the same direction makes a track or path. In the same way, the more often we do anything in the same way or simultaneously, the more we shall be inclined to do it. At last, a habit is formed.

Why is it easy to form bad habits and so hard to form good ones? The reason is very simple. Our natural inclination is to take the line of least resistance. It requires, at first, a special effort to take the more difficult of two possible courses of action.

For instance, it is easier to lie in bed on a cold morning than to get up early. It is easier to tell a lie than own up and take the punishment for a fault. It is easier to put off today's duties to tomorrow than to do them at the right time. Now a habit is formed by repetition. Every time we yield to temptation makes it easier to yield and more challenging to resist the next time. So we form the habits of laziness, lying, and unpunctuality.

Happily, good habits are formed in the same way. The forming of good habits calls for effort and determination at first, but every time we resist temptation and do what is wise and good in the long run, we make the subsequent struggle less severe. At last, we form a good habit, which would be hard to break even if we wanted to break it. Get into the habit of early rising, and you will not want to lie in bed like a lazy bone.

Experts say that the best way to form a new habit is to tie it to an existing habit. So, observe the patterns in your day and think about how you can use existing habits to create new, positive ones.

For many of us, our morning routine is our strongest routine, so that is a great place to attach a new habit. A morning cup of coffee, for example, can create an excellent opportunity to start a new one-minute meditation practice. Or, while brushing your teeth, you can start walking for five minutes immediately after.

Dr. B.J. Fogg, the author of the book "Tiny Habits," described that big behavior change requires a high level of motivation that often cannot be sustained. He suggested starting with tiny habits to make the new habit as easy as possible in the beginning. For example, a daily short walk could be the beginning of an exercise habit or putting an apple in your bag every day could lead to better eating habits.

In his own life, Dr. Fogg started with just two push-ups a day and, to make the habit stick, tied his push-ups to a daily habit of going to the bathroom. He began after a bathroom trip by doing two push-ups. Now he has a habit of 40 to 80 push-ups a day.

British researchers who published the study in the European Journal of Social Psychology showed that the amount of time it took for the task to become a habit ranged from 18 to 254 days. The median time was 66 days. The habits take a long time to create, but they form faster when you practice them more often, so start with something easy to do.

Obstacles come in the path of habit formation. Habit researchers know people are more likely to form new habits when they clear away the obstacles that stand in their way.

**Focus on one habit at a time**

In general, while people think about transforming their lives, they often set gigantic goals for themselves and try to achieve them as quickly as possible. This way of doing things fails because it requires very strict self-discipline and monk-like willpower. Willpower is a finite resource; it depletes over time. So, it shows real challenges every day, and after some time, people give up. Instead, you should focus totally on one thing, and intentions get diluted if you try to improve multiple habits at the same time. Habit becomes more automatic with more practice. On average, it takes at least two months for new habits to become automatic behaviors. It is better to focus on one specific habit, work on it until you master it, and make it an automatic part of your daily life. Then, repeat the process for the next habit. The way to master more things, in the long run, is to focus on one thing right now.

One of the hardest things for many people when it comes to building new habits is not to take on too many at once. When people first start out, they want to build several habits at once. Every time they have tried that approach, they end up failing. Usually, a few of the habits don't stick, but sometimes none of them do. It's just too much to focus on, a bit like multitasking, where your brain has to constantly switch contexts because you really can't focus on multiple things at once.

You will become overwhelmed and lose momentum with any good habits if you try to take on too much at a time. Your dream may shudder at the beginning itself if you expect to see complete change overnight. Because of this, it's so important to begin with, small steps when you are integrating new, healthy habits into your life. If you go all-in right away and tire yourself out too much, you are way more likely to burn yourself out and become discouraged if you don't see results right away or if you weren't able to complete the whole workout due to exhaustion.

It's a good idea to remember the intention and purpose that you set when you began your journey of instilling your new habit. Doing this will help you confirm if you're still going in the direction you want to, and you can change your course of action if required. This will surely help you stay on track with your habits and will allow staying even more in tune with yourself.

When you are committed to building good habits in your life, it's essential to understand that there will be many challenges and roadblocks ahead to building a new habit. Life throws surprises, and things come up out of the blue as well as unforeseen circumstances, but that is just a part of life. It's important to remember that it's okay if you "fail" once in a while and that this does not negate all the hard work you have put in.

To ensure you are persistent with your good habits is to come up with a reward system for yourself. The reward needs to be something that will promote the new habit that you are trying to form and not take away or inhibit the progress. It's also important to remember to celebrate any small wins, such as successfully going a full day or week incorporating your new habit into your routine.

**Build Awareness**

It is essential to start your new habit by building awareness. Wear a rubber band in your hand for a month. Every time your brain thinks of going back to the habit, hit yourself hard with the rubber band. Every time you go through pain, your brain looks for the cause. If the cause is simultaneous and consistent, it will associate that cause with pain. You do it enough, and you will fool your brain into believing that the mere thought of the habit would give you pain. Pay attention to your current habits and identify one that you want to change in some way. All change begins with making choices. What habits do you like? Which habits are you willing to take steps to change?

Attach a new habit or behavior to something you already do regularly. One strategy you can use is to connect a new habit with an existing habit. For example: if you want to begin sit-ups, plan to do it just after visiting the toilet. To start mindfulness in your routine, you might select a time immediately after brushing your teeth each morning.

Gain clarity about what you want to do and how you will do it. Be specific and bite off just a tiny chunk. Start with a simple step. Let yourself know that a tiny step at a time can add up to powerful new habits and behaviors. James Clear recommends "the two-minute rule" as you begin a new habit. Break the habit into a small enough chunk that it can be accomplished in two minutes or less. Remember the "why." Keeping in mind why we're doing something – the personal value, meaning, and importance of a behavior can be helpful.

**Set micro habits**

In the spirit of keeping things simple, another option is to try out micro habits. Incremental achievements move you closer to achieving your goals. Think of them like stepping-stones that lead to your final destination. A big mistake a lot of people make when building habits generally is that their habits are actually collections of habits.

Many people want to get in the habit of writing every morning, which is a great habit, but the tricky part is that writing every morning may involve multiple steps, which could be thought of as a "micro-habit."

But writing every morning may require getting up earlier than usual, then do all your morning routines first. Then, once that foundation is established, you can start writing every morning. This technique is especially important if you have the added pressure of a hectic schedule since you may not have the time or energy to work on bigger, multi-step habits.

The principle is simple if you focus on one small habit at a time, you'll be able to achieve your goals in a much easier and sustainable way. Let's retake the weight loss example. If your goal is to lose weight, you can start by focusing on one habit, for example, eliminating the fat-rich products from your breakfast every day from your diet. After the instillation of this habit, you can add on another habit; for example, add half an hour of walking to your daily routine. Once this is completed, you can start going to the gym for one hour every weekend. Stet by step, changing your habits will ensure a natural and sustainable change.

It is important to keep each habit reasonable to maintain momentum and make the behavior as easy as possible to accomplish. If you want to build up 20 minutes of meditation, then split it into two segments of 10 minutes at first. If you are trying to do 50 push-ups per day, five sets of 10 might be much easier as you make your way there.

**Prepare for challenges**

It is inevitable to find thousands of challenges to developing good habits. You should be mentally preparing for those challenges so that you can easily overcome them.

When the intention is strong, any obstacle becomes weaker. You should reflect on why you want this habit—the stronger the 'why,' easier to build habits. So, whenever anything stops you from developing habits, you should remember the why.

You need to find an accountability partner to share your goals to keep yourself accountable. Research shows that your odds of success dramatically increase when you make your intentions known to someone perceived to have a higher status than yourself or someone whose opinion you value.

**Schedule and track your habits**

Life is busy and hectic, and overwhelming. Whether you have been living with no schedule *at all* or you usually attempt to make a schedule but rarely stick to it, there are a few things to keep in mind to ensure you will be successful in creating and sticking to your plans.

The hardest part about sticking to a schedule is getting started and becoming used to that sense of commitment. You need to give yourself some motivation to start this new method of being productive by choosing some things that you would be excited about changing.

In general, it takes anywhere between 21 days to 66 days to form a new habit. This means that once you start making your schedule, you have to give yourself time to adjust to sticking to it so you can be sure that you're allowing yourself a fair chance to succeed. This time will also allow you to make any necessary tweaks to your schedule to make it easy for you to stick to. Sometimes, your first schedule doesn't work out. You should remember that your daily schedule is meant to benefit you, so go ahead and tweak away.

Therefore, you need to make a schedule to practice the behavior you want to build into a habit. Be sure not to overdo it initially because if you dive in too fast and expect results right away, you will likely fail and become discouraged at the beginning only.

So, start small and do it consistently to imprint it in your subconscious mind. When things get imprinted in the subconscious mind consistently, it builds habits over time. That is required to build long-term momentum for success.

People who do small work consistently over time yield better results than those who do hard work inconsistently and for a short period.

# Final Words

Thank you for reading this book. I hope that this has been helpful to you to get over bad habits and replace them with good habits. Good habits are powerful. Building good habits help you grow personally and professionally. It might seem formidable at first when attempting to work better habits into your lifestyle, but the most challenging part is often taking the initial step and beginning the process once and for all. The fact that you have become aware of changes that you'd like to make and are considering working towards making those changes is phenomenal and deserves its own recognition. Creating healthier habits for yourself is a fantastic way to improve your mental health, and when you look back after some time, you will be so glad that you began the journey when you did.

The next step is to ensure that you are practicing all these and reaffirm that you are on your way to becoming a better, fuller you every day. The key to success is consistency and determination. Believe in yourself and your ability to develop new habits necessary to realize your goals. Once you start replacing your bad habits with good ones, you are on the right track to success.

There are many benefits to learning how to build habits. This book has covered many important aspects of the habit-building process, from replacing bad habits to starting new habits.

Besides, it also covered the importance of building habits and the everyday habits of successful people.

In addition to being a great reference book for students who desire to be successful, it also provides an excellent source for those who want to improve their habits. The book has also elaborated on how to get rid of bad habits and how to develop new habits.

This book has described thoroughly the process of breaking bad habits and building good habits. If you want to see yourself at the next level, you need to commit to improving your habits. You might already have some of the habits mentioned in this book, but real transformation will occur when you strengthen your good habits and inculcate new habits. "Excellent habits are the key to an excellent life."

To succeed and end well in life, there's a need to discard those bad habits and consciously build the right habit. Build those habits that will bring about your desired success. Persisting in a bad habit and expecting its outcome to turn good magically is foolishness in disguise.

Good habits are essential for making progress in everyday life and making success. If you have good habits and follow them every day, then there is nothing you should be worrying about. Good luck.

# Could You Help?

I'd love to hear your opinion about my book. In the world of book publishing, more valuable are the honest reviews from a wide variety of readers.

Your review will help other readers determine whether my book is for them. It will also help me reach more readers by increasing the visibility of my book. Therefore, I sincerely request you to directly leave your review on this platform.

Thanks for supporting my work.

# Disclaimer

Although the publisher and the author have made every effort to ensure that the information in this book is correct, and while this publication is designed to provide accurate information regarding the subject matter covered, the publisher and the author assume no responsibility for errors, inaccuracies, omissions, or any other inconsistencies herein and hereby disclaim any liability to any party for any loss, damage, or disruption caused by errors or omissions, and whether such errors or omissions result from negligence, accident, or any other cause.

The ideas, procedures, and suggestions in this book are not intended as a substitute for consulting with an expert. Neither the author nor the publisher shall be liable or responsible for any loss or damage allegedly arising from any information or suggestion in this book.

Names, characters, and incidents in this book are either the product of the author's imagination or used in a fictitious manner. Any resemblance to an actual person, living or dead, or actual events is purely coincidental.

# COPYRIGHT © 2022 PRADIP N DAS

# Gratitude

This book is dedicated to all the readers around the Globe who inspire me to continue on the writer's journey.

I sincerely thank the Almighty and all my well-wishers, who supported me with their love and appreciation.

Jn

---

[1] https://www.speakingtree.in/blog/the-touchstone

# Also by Pradip N Das

**Success Plan for Youth**
Teenagers' Guide To Success


**Standalone**
Success Strategy for Students
Seven Essential Skills to Success
The Power of Attitude in Success
Building Mental Strength For Success
7 Best Sacrifices To Success
The Art of Managing Success
The Power of Reading
Steps to Design Your Life
Building Habits